Early Interventions in Reading

SRA

Level 1

Activity Book C

Columbus, OH

The **McGraw·Hill** Companies

SRAonline.com

 SRA

Send all inquiries to:
SRA/McGraw-Hill
4400 Easton Commons
Columbus, OH 43219

Printed in the United States of America.

ISBN 0-07-602663-9

8 9 10 11 12 13   VHG   12 11 10 09

Table of Contents

Name_____

Lesson 81

Activity 4

_____   _____
- - - - - - - - - - - - - - - - -   - - - - - - - - - - - - - - - - -
_____   _____
- - - - - - - - - - - - - - - - -   - - - - - - - - - - - - - - - - -
_____   _____
- - - - - - - - - - - - - - - - -   - - - - - - - - - - - - - - - - -
_____   _____

Activity 6

_____   _____   _____   _____
- - - e - - -   - - - - - - -   - - - - - - -   - - - - - - -
_____   _____   _____   _____
- - - o - - -   - - - - - - -   - - - - - - -   - - - - - - -

Lesson 82

Activity 4

<u>cr</u>ut<u>ch</u>es

<u>s</u>and<u>w</u>ich

<u>k</u>it<u>ch</u>en

<u>un</u>der

<u>un</u>der<u>s</u>tand

<u>g</u>lit<u>t</u>er

Activity Book C

Lesson 83

Activity 3

<u>dish</u>es   <u>plas</u>t<u>i</u>c   <u>fish</u><u>net</u>

<u>car</u>p<u>et</u>   <u>splin</u>t<u>er</u>   <u>car</u>p<u>en</u>t<u>er</u>

<u>gar</u>d<u>en</u>   <u>box</u><u>es</u>

Activity 4

<u>Patches and Dan</u>

1. Dan pitches the stick.

2. Patches wants to catch it.

3. The stick splashes into the pond.

4. Patches fetches the stick.

_____ _____ _____ _____

Lesson 83

Activity 5

_dge

fudge

edge

judge

badge

Activity Book C

Lesson 83

Activity 6

trash	drum	flag
stash	split	then
bench	scrap	lunch
children		garden
fishnet		dented

Activity 7

half	three	five
two	four	one

Lesson 84

Activity 2

Activity 3

Lesson 84

Activity 5

<u>mar</u>ket   <u>ca</u>n<u>n</u>ot

<u>wi</u>s<u>h</u>es   <u>ni</u>c<u>k</u>el

<u>ga</u>r<u>d</u>en   <u>c</u>hi<u>ck</u>en

Activity 6

I'_

_ o _ ay

Lesson 85

Activity 1

_____   _____
- - - - - - - - - - - - - - - -   - - - - - - - - - - - - - - - -
_____   _____

_____   _____
- - - - - - - - - - - - - - - -   - - - - - - - - - - - - - - - -
_____   _____

Lesson 85

Activity 3

_dge   a_e   p   k   ea

j   or   al   f   h   e

wh   y   le   z   ur   u

r   ing   er   ch   w   l

tch   th   x   c   ar   ck

b   sh   o   g   ir   c   r

Activity Book C

9

Lesson 85

Activity 6

lamp   lad   first

back   with   costs

sell   full   a<u>sk</u>ed

scra<u>tch</u>   <u>nickel</u>   <u>scratch</u>ed

Activity 7

of   said   do

have   today   be

we   he   she   does

Activity Book C

Name_____

Lesson 86

Activity 4

Lesson 86

Activity 5

1. Ren has a _____ on her head.

| cap |
| cape |

2. Pat fixed her model _____ _____ .

| plan |
| plane |

3. A whale _____ swim.

| can |
| cane |

4. Mark _____ muffins.

| mad |
| made |

5. Kate has a _____ kitten.

| fat |
| fate |

Lesson 86

Activity 6

ey

ere

Activity 7

called   watch   lake

snake   shade   wade

awake   waded   mistake

fish   shape   things

crossed

Lesson 87

Activity 2

sn<u>a</u>ke	mad
cr<u>a</u>ne	made
h<u>i</u>de	rip
<u>a</u>ge	ripe
p<u>a</u>ge	Tim
c<u>a</u>ke	time

Activity 3

<u>ee</u>

m<u>ee</u>t	f<u>ee</u>t	k<u>ee</u>p
sl<u>ee</u>p	wh<u>ee</u>l	b<u>ee</u>
j<u>ee</u>p	thr<u>ee</u>	s<u>ee</u>
sh<u>ee</u>p	f<u>ee</u>l	w<u>ee</u>d

 Activity Book C

Lesson 87

Activity 4

yes/no

_____

1. A woman sits on a chair. _____

2. A plane lands in the grass. _____

3. Nate swims in the lake. _____

4. A cat tastes the grapes. _____

5. A dog wins the race. _____

6. A plane is in the air. _____

Lesson 88

Activity 2

J<u>a</u>ne   <u>j</u>ar   t<u>i</u>de

<u>j</u>abbed   t<u>a</u>ke   n<u>i</u>ne

ri<u>dg</u>e   <u>j</u>et   litt<u>l</u>e

ba<u>ck</u>   d<u>i</u>me   <u>g</u>entle

Activity 3

s<u>ea</u>t   <u>ea</u>ch   <u>ea</u>t

m<u>ea</u>t   b<u>ea</u>ch

b<u>ea</u>ns   <u>ea</u>gle

     Activity Book C

Lesson 88

Activity 4

<u>un</u>der	<u>fin</u>ish
es<u>cap</u>e	<u>gig</u>antic
<u>kitch</u>en	<u>milkshake</u>

Activity 5

Lesson 89

Activity 2

_____

- -

_____

_____

- -

_____

_____

- -

_____

Activity 5

<u>wh</u>en   tr<u>i</u>p   p<u>a</u>ge

c<u>a</u>pe   h<u>u</u>nt   l<u>ar</u>ge

Activity 6

ma<u>g</u>ic   <u>batt</u>le   <u>blaze</u>s

<u>e</u>s<u>c</u>ape   <u>came</u>ls   <u>g</u>ira<u>ffe</u>s

    Activity Book C

Lesson 90

Activity 2

_____   _____
---------------------------------   ---------------------------------
_____   _____
_____   _____
---------------------------------   ---------------------------------
_____   _____
_____   _____
---------------------------------   ---------------------------------
_____   _____
---------------------------------   ---------------------------------
_____   _____

Activity 3

p<u>ar</u>ade   <u>in</u>side

<u>Emm</u>a   <u>A</u>pril

<u>K</u>amar<u>a</u>   wa<u>go</u>n

Lesson 90

Activity 7

minds   finds   shed

heads   kite   path

white   bike   all   same

Activity 9

the on have she was I'm

are he has with what here to

you there said for says away

does one two could five should

three out want eight four do

be hurry water today they were

would hurray no of my

Activity Book C

Lesson 91

_____

s

ce

ci

Activity 2

cent _____   circus _____

cider _____   space _____

Gran likes nice mice.

_____

We danced in a circle.

_____

Lesson 91

Activity 3

ce	**ci**
fa<u>c</u>e	<u>c</u>ider
i<u>c</u>e	<u>c</u>ircle
ri<u>c</u>e	<u>c</u>ircu<u>s</u>
mi<u>c</u>e	

Activity 5

1. I like to _____ a bike.

2. Did you _____ the page?

3. Kate is gentle _____ and _____ .

rid
ride

rip
ripe

kin
kind

Activity Book C

Lesson 91

Activity 7

f<u>i</u>ne	sm<u>i</u>les	k<u>i</u>te
par<u>a</u>de	s<u>a</u>ved	r<u>i</u>des
tr<u>i</u>ke	sh<u>e</u>d	<u>a</u>fter
br<u>i</u>dge	h<u>ea</u>d	sp<u>i</u>ke
wh<u>i</u>ne	l<u>a</u>ke	h<u>i</u>m

Lesson 92

Activity 3

_____   _____
_   _
_____   _____
_   _
_____   _____
_   _
_____   _____
_   _
_____   _____

Activity 5

plate	nut	chop	date
nine	shake	pinch	that
slice	ripe	spice	cake

Lesson 92

Activity 6

yes/no

1. Jen hides behind a bike. _____

2. Nine mice ride a bike. _____

3. A chimp licks grape ice. _____

4. The twins ride a slide. _____

5. Tish has a kite. _____

6. A fish smiles at the child. _____

Lesson 93

Activity 3

go	home
so	tone
no	shone
	note

open
___

protect
___

program
___

Activity 4

this	plate	pinch
shake	nuts	chop
chopped	chopping	

Lesson 93

Activity 5

make	spice	save
can	taste	and
slice	stir	then
like	while	nice
ripe	help	date

Lesson 94

Activity 2

<u>sp</u>i<u>d</u>er   <u>in</u><u>sec</u>ts   <u>g</u>ar<u>d</u>en   <u>u</u>n<u>ti</u>l

<u>br</u>i<u>dg</u>es   <u>a</u>like   <u>si</u>s<u>t</u>er

<u>p</u>i<u>r</u>ate   <u>dra</u>g<u>l</u>ine   <u>wonderful</u>

Activity 3

g<u>ir</u>ls   Gra<u>c</u>e   thr<u>ea</u>d   cl<u>u</u>b

<u>l</u>o<u>t</u>s   y<u>e</u>s   j<u>u</u>mps   <u>wh</u>ich

b<u>ar</u>n   m<u>a</u>de   s<u>i</u>lk   n<u>e</u>xt   <u>y</u>elled

Activity 4

ese

ose

Lesson 95

Activity 1

ur	ce	s	ck	ir
gi	ci	i_e	ea	ee
ge	a_e	al	or	y
ch	le	tch	_dge	o_e

Activity 3

ere	o e	wo
ou	eigh	a
ere	ou	
ere	y	ai

Activity Book C

Lesson 95

V

Activity 4

v

vine _____ van _____

brave _____ five _____

Victor has seven valentines.

Lesson 95

Activity 4

van	vet
silver	drive
seven	visit
never	vase

Lesson 97

Activity 1

ol	v	o_e	ce	ol
a_e	j	r	f	d
gi	ar	ck	sh	tch
ing	ir	th	o_e	ol

Activity 2

_____ _____

- - - - - - - - - - - - - - - - - - - - - - - - - -

_____ _____

- - - - - - - - - - - - - - - - - - - - - - - - - -

_____ _____

- - - - - - - - - - - - - - - - - - - - - - - - - -

_____ _____

- - - - - - - - - - - - - - - - - - - - - - - - - -

_____ _____

Activity Book C

Lesson 97

Activity 4

_____   _____

o

Activity 5

h<u>o</u>me   r<u>o</u>be   n<u>o</u>se

<u>o</u>n   m<u>o</u>le   n<u>o</u>t

<u>i</u>ce   n<u>o</u>te   t<u>a</u>ke

m<u>a</u>de   st<u>o</u>ne   h<u>e</u>lp

Lesson 98

Activity 2

_____ _____
- - - - - - - - - - - - - - - - - - - - - - - - - - - - - - - -
_____ _____
- - - - - - - - - - - - - - - - - - - - - - - - - - - - - - - -
_____ _____
- - - - - - - - - - - - - - - - - - - - - - - - - - - - - - - -
_____ _____

Activity 5

problem   perfect

forest   suppose

outside   baskets

pocket   acorn

secret

Lesson 99

Activity 3

be	pet	she	we
cold	bugs	me	red
will	stone	shade	for

Activity 4

huge	bugs	mule	pipe
trade	trades		trader
branch	branches		budge
use	used		push

Lesson 99

Activity 5

<u>secret</u>	<u>refuse</u>
<u>fore</u>st	<u>mu</u>sic
<u>riv</u>er	<u>ani</u>mals
<u>Alfon</u>so	<u>a</u>muse
<u>Ama</u>zon	<u>bas</u>kets
Cup<u>i</u>d	

Activity Book C

Lesson 100

Activity 1

Lesson 100

Activity 4

stove	drives	never
velvet	saves	vase

1. My mom _____ a van.

2. Jim _____ baseball cards.

3. Val has a _____ dress.

4. Lance put the pan on the _____.

5. Put the roses in a _____.

Lesson 100

Activity 7

have   onto   was   today

I'm   are   what   does

here   to   you   there   my

said   oh   says   away   of

one   two   could   should

three   out   want   eight

four   do   half   hurry   water

they   were   would   hurray

those   once   wrote   these

oh no   where   pull   put

Lesson 101

Activity 4

s<u>e</u>cr<u>et</u>	p<u>o</u>ck<u>e</u>t
<u>a</u>corn	dr<u>a</u>g<u>o</u>n
dr<u>a</u>g<u>o</u>ns	t<u>e</u>rr<u>i</u>ble
t<u>i</u>ck<u>le</u>d	l<u>i</u>tt<u>le</u>
<u>e</u>v<u>e</u>n	f<u>e</u>v<u>e</u>r

Name_____

Lesson 102

Activity 1

a_e   ea   ee   ai   ge

ck   ce   e_e   _ay   e

gi_   ci_   ur   y   a   i

Activity 5

face   steps   these   moped

so   head   go   huge   hard

just   smiled   those   front

Activity 6

Hugo   Nana   invite   even

Eva   able   problem   inside

dragon   today   behind

Lesson 103

Activity 2

○ The giraffe has a long neck.

○ Eve runs from the giraffe.

○ The man is on skates.

○ The man is on a trapeze.

○ We sat on the fence.

○ We put a dime in the meter.

Lesson 103

Activity 3

_____

- -

_____

Activity 5

_____   _____

- - - - - - - - - - - - - -   - - - - - - - - - - - - - -

_____   _____

_____   _____

- - - - - - - - - - - - - -   - - - - - - - - - - - - - -

_____   _____

_____   _____

- - - - - - - - - - - - - -   - - - - - - - - - - - - - -

_____   _____

_____   _____

- - - - - - - - - - - - - -   - - - - - - - - - - - - - -

_____   _____

Lesson 104

Activity 1

e<u>a</u>t   m<u>ai</u>l   dr<u>ea</u>m   c<u>o</u>lds   bette<u>r</u>

Sunda<u>y</u>   cr<u>ea</u>k   ch<u>ee</u>k   tick<u>le</u>   sp<u>ea</u>k

t<u>ea</u>   f<u>ee</u>l   q<u>u</u>ick   sh<u>ar</u>k   p<u>a</u>ls

Activity 2

dr<u>a</u>g<u>o</u>ns   ter<u>ri</u>ble   sn<u>ee</u>z<u>i</u>ng

q<u>u</u>i<u>e</u>t   ma<u>i</u>nt<u>ai</u>n

<u>an</u>k<u>le</u>   pl<u>a</u>y<u>e</u>r

Activity 3

_____   _____   _____

_____   _____   _____

_____   _____   _____

_____   _____   _____

Lesson 105

Activity 2

<u>q</u>ueen   s<u>q</u>uid   s<u>ea</u>

f<u>ea</u>st   m<u>ea</u>l   squ<u>ea</u>l

hu<u>g</u>e   li<u>q</u>uid   aw<u>ay</u>

Lesson 106

Activity 1

ci   qu   ai   qu   ce   ay

ear   ing   tch   ai   z   qu

gi   a_e   ee   u   qu   ay

ci   sh   th   ce   ai   qu

Activity 2

Activity Book C

Lesson 106

Activity 5

dr<u>ea</u>m   du<u>c</u>k   gr<u>ee</u>n

und<u>e</u>r   l<u>ea</u>ves   sa<u>v</u>ed

<u>s</u>hark   s<u>ea</u>   s<u>q</u>uid

qu<u>i</u>te   <u>qu</u>it   hu<u>g</u>e

fa<u>ce</u>   asl<u>ee</u>p

d<u>a</u>rk   hurr<u>a</u>y

Lesson 107

Activity 1

ee	ear	ay	ai	qu
i_e	eer	ay	qu	_y
ge	ur	eer	ear	u_e
y	ai	er	ir	ce

Activity 3

m<u>ai</u>l	<u>qu</u>ack	rep<u>ea</u>t
b<u>a</u>rked	dr<u>ea</u>ms	stor<u>y</u>
fl<u>ea</u>s	b<u>ee</u>s	ne<u>x</u>t
ch<u>a</u>se	awa<u>y</u>	<u>sh</u>eep
litt<u>le</u>	<u>h</u>ear	h<u>ur</u>ry

Activity Book C

Lesson 107

Activity 4

_o _ e

_our

_

Activity 5

s<u>ai</u>l	d<u>ay</u>	F<u>ay</u>
R<u>ay</u>	b<u>ai</u>l	r<u>ai</u>n
tod<u>ay</u>	w<u>ai</u>t	m<u>ai</u>n
b<u>ai</u>t	afr<u>ai</u>d	st<u>ay</u>
r<u>ai</u>se	s<u>ai</u>ling	

Lesson 108

Activity 4

dr<u>ea</u>ms	<u>Qu</u>incy	qua<u>ck</u>
<u>qu</u>acked	rep<u>ea</u>t	h<u>urr</u>y
sp<u>o</u>ke	sl<u>ee</u>p	w<u>a</u>ke
<u>th</u>ree	stor<u>y</u>	st<u>o</u>ries
l<u>ea</u>ves	fl<u>ea</u>s	t<u>i</u>red

Activity Book C

Lesson 109

Activity 1

ear	ur	_y	qu	a_e
ai	ge	ci	z	ee
_dge	a_e	v	ol	al
tch	r	i	a	e_e

Activity 4

dreamers   dreaming   Quincy
‗‗‗‗‗‗‗‗   ‗‗ ‗‗ ‗‗   ‗‗ ‗‗

duckling   opossum   table
‗‗ ‗‗ ‗‗   ‗‗ ‗‗ ‗‗   ‗‗ ‗‗

napkins   puppies   every
‗‗ ‗‗ ‗‗   ‗‗ ‗‗ ‗‗   ‗‗ ‗‗

invited   begins   ribbons
‗‗ ‗‗ ‗‗   ‗‗ ‗‗   ‗‗ ‗‗ ‗‗

Lesson 110

Activity 1

ci	ch	ck	ce	c
ai	_are	_y	sh	o_e
qu	_ay	ee	ce	c
gi	al	d	b	u_e
tch	th	r	ur	ir

Activity 2

_____ _____ _____

_____ _____ _____

_____ _____ _____

_____ _____ _____

_____ _____ _____

_____

Activity Book C

Lesson 110

Activity 3

scare	squirrel	umpire	store
deer	more	scored	square

1. A _____ is in
the nut tree.

2. May I have _____ time?

3. Beth _____ three home runs.

4. Tam got her jacket at the _____.

5. A _____ has four equal sides.

6. The _____ was at the
baseball game.

Lesson 110

Activity 5

p<u>ar</u>ty	p<u>ar</u>ties
fanc<u>y</u>	fanc<u>i</u>er
tedd<u>y</u>	tedd<u>ie</u>s
ever<u>y</u>	pl<u>ea</u>se
m<u>ore</u>	b<u>e</u>gins
<u>ice</u>	cr<u>ea</u>m
tab<u>le</u>	

Activity Book C

Lesson 110

Activity 6

Oh   half   Mr.   where

pull   was   are   have

Mrs.   here   what   to

you   there   put   said   those

says   away   of   does   one

two   wrote   could   onto   would

out   four   want   eight   should

oh no   hurry   my   water

do   I'm   these   today

they   were   once   heard   some

your   bear

Lesson 111

i
_igh
i_e

Activity 1

high _____ sigh _____

sight _____ flight _____

The light is bright.

_____

You may be right.

_____

Lesson 111

Activity 2

cherry

basket

dragon

city

candle

queen

baby

prince

Lesson 111

Activity 3

pl<u>ai</u>n   prin<u>ce</u>   cra<u>y</u>on

c<u>are</u>   <u>ch</u>air   sw<u>ee</u>t

<u>c</u>enter   pap<u>er</u>   <u>le</u>ave

Nell<u>ie</u>   cr<u>ea</u>m   di<u>r</u>ty

Activity 4

b<u>e</u><u>gin</u>   b<u>e</u><u>ginn</u>ing

<u>summe</u>r   mem<u>o</u><u>ry</u>

<u>mail</u><u>man</u>   <u>day</u><u>dream</u>

<u>yes</u><u>ter</u><u>day</u>   <u>com</u><u>pu</u>ter

<u>every</u><u>day</u>   <u>pa</u>per

Lesson 112

Activity 2

w<u>a</u>ke   b<u>ir</u>ds   c<u>a</u>ll   hi<u>gh</u>

d<u>ay</u>   br<u>igh</u>t   ret<u>ur</u>n   pl<u>ay</u>

b<u>a</u>bies   n<u>igh</u>t   sl<u>ee</u>p   h<u>o</u>ld

Activity 3

_ _ ai _   _____

_ o _ _ _ _ _   _____

Name _____

Lesson 112

Activity 4

r<u>eturns</u>   to<u>night</u>   <u>babies</u>

<u>opossum</u>   <u>beginner</u>   <u>ins</u>ects

<u>daylight</u>   <u>thunder</u>   <u>frighten</u>

<u>lightbulb</u>   <u>high chair</u>   spider

Activity 5

_____
- - - - - - - - - - - -
_____
- - - - - - - - - - - -
_____
- - - - - - - - - - - -
_____
- - - - - - - - - - - -

_____
- - - - - - - - - - - -
_____
- - - - - - - - - - - -
_____
- - - - - - - - - - - -
_____
- - - - - - - - - - - -

Activity Book C

Name _____

Lesson 112

Activity 7

 1. See the _____
run.

deer
dean

 2. Mom _____
leaves.

racks
rakes

 3. A whale swims in the
_____
_____.

sea
seal

 4. I eat _____ for
dinner.

meat
mean

 5. The dog does a
_____
_____.

flea
flip

Lesson 113

Activity 3

fly	tie	tries	pie	sky

1. The _____ buzzes on my head.

2. I made the cherry _____ by myself.

3. Spot _____ to do a trick.

Activity 4

r<u>ai</u>ned   ni<u>gh</u>t   p<u>ai</u>nt   hi<u>gh</u>

swin<u>g</u>   <u>ch</u>ildren   bett<u>er</u>   <u>ea</u>gle

ret<u>ur</u>ning   w<u>a</u>ke   b<u>ir</u>ds   <u>sh</u>ine

cit<u>y</u>   sn<u>ai</u>l   afr<u>ai</u>d   lett<u>er</u>s

Lesson 113

Activity 5

popcorn

thirsty

unhappy

library

twenty

emergency

memory

fifty

seaweed

Lesson 113

Activity 6

ponies	thirsty	twenty
emergency	stories	cherries

1. Popcorn can make you _____.

2. Call Dad in an _____.

3. Jenny likes to eat sweet _____.

4. Thirty is more than _____.

5. The _____ were nice to ride.

6. There are many _____ to read in the library.

Activity Book C

Lesson 114

Activity 3

_____

pony = _____

penny = _____

es   lily = _____

try = _____

fly = _____

fancy = _____

thirsty = _____

er   happy = _____

funny = _____

Lesson 114

Activity 5

Bl**y**	bet**ter**	sta**y**
dr**y**	ostri**ch**	sm**all**
anim**a**ls	**ea**gle	sk**y**
m**y**self	l**ie**	repl**ie**s
sti**ck**	tr**ee**s	l**i**on
	chimp	

Lesson 115

Activity 2

ay	igh	ce	c	x
ch	ge	ol	ear	igh
_y	ai	igh	ur	sh
z	b	ck	al	ing
qu	igh	y	wh	igh

Activity 3

Lesson 115

Activity 4

p<u>l</u>ate	m<u>ea</u>n
<u>wh</u>ite	<u>squ</u>eeze
s<u>ea</u>weed	<u>v</u>isit
p<u>ay</u>	sn<u>ai</u>l
tr<u>y</u>	fi<u>ng</u>er
f<u>ar</u>mer	alwa<u>y</u>s
ever<u>y</u>	stri<u>ng</u>

Lesson 115

_ng

Activity 6

wing _____   thing _____

ring _____   spring _____

The king rang a gong.

We sang a long song.

Lesson 116

Activity 1

igh	ing	ay	ee	er
ai	x	z	ol	qu
igh	u_e	tch	_dge	th
ong	ear	ce	ur	ck
ang	_y	b	are	_ng

Activity 3

thund<u>er</u>	br<u>igh</u>t	cr<u>y</u>	n<u>ee</u>ds
<u>f</u><u>ar</u>mer	d<u>ar</u>k	ch<u>a</u>se	<u>b</u><u>ank</u>
<u>H</u><u>an</u>k	q<u>u</u>een	<u>sh</u>eep	bo<u>x</u>es
hold<u>ing</u>	tr<u>ai</u>n	cl<u>er</u>k

Lesson 116

Activity 4

chunking

robber

farmer

hotbox

jumping

honking

racket

blanket

cranky

judge

something

police

teacher

Lesson 116

Activity 5

1. Can you hear the girls _____?

sing   sink

2. When I am sick, it is hard to _____.

thing   think

3. _____ the blanket to the baby.

Bring   Brink

4. The bird's right _____ is hurt.

wing   wink

5. I lost the _____ from my finger.

ring   rink

6. The monkey can _____ to the vine.

cling   clink

Activity Book C

Lesson 116

Activity 6

sell	time	Hank
honk	honked	hissed
hissing	chased	kept
police	lamp	very
over	bank	thanked

Lesson 117

Activity 2

Name _____

Lesson 117

Activity 3

crazy   dragon   sky   car

wheel   cute   nice   paint

muddy   grand   letter   kitten

uncle   rice   eating

Activity 4

_____   _____

- - - - - - - - - - - - - - - - - -   - - - - - - - - - - - - - - - - - -

_____   _____

- - - - - - - - - - - - - - - - - -   - - - - - - - - - - - - - - - - - -

_____   _____

- - - - - - - - - - - - - - - - - -   - - - - - - - - - - - - - - - - - -

_____   _____

- - - - - - - - - - - - - - - - - -   - - - - - - - - - - - - - - - - - -

_____   _____

Activity Book C

Lesson 117

Activity 5

paint _____   _____

bake _____   _____

slip _____   _____

rule _____   _____

Activity 6

<u>h</u>i<u>g</u>h<u>w</u>ay   <u>whacker</u>   <u>g</u>rand<u>s</u>on

<u>checking</u>   <u>sending</u>   <u>thinking</u>

<u>thanking</u>   <u>thankful</u>   <u>thankfull</u>y

<u>deliver</u>   <u>eating</u>

Lesson 118

Activity 1

ing	er	qu	igh	ai
f	i	i_e	ir	a
a_e	e	e_e	u	u_e
ch	le	_dge	v	ce
ck	x	igh	_y	ear
ong	ang	_ay	eer	ol

Activity 2

1. We like fresh cherries.

2. Six logs were on the fire.

3. That little fly tickles me.

4. Nick has a pink necktie.

5. The baby will cry if she is sleepy.

6. A flashlight will help you see in the dark.

Lesson 118

Activity 4

read<u>ing</u>	qua<u>ck</u>	sn<u>ai</u>l	h<u>o</u>lds
bo<u>x</u>	car<u>r</u>y	car<u>r</u>ies	<u>th</u>is
s<u>e</u>nt	sp<u>ee</u>d	speed<u>y</u>	mi<u>gh</u>t
stro<u>ng</u>	bri<u>ng</u>	r<u>ai</u>ned	

Activity 5

<u>hot</u><u>box</u>	<u>some</u><u>one</u>	<u>whack</u><u>er</u>
<u>send</u><u>ing</u>	<u>grand</u><u>son</u>	<u>tick</u><u>ets</u>
<u>check</u><u>ing</u>	<u>fix</u><u>ing</u>	<u>fix</u><u>es</u>
<u>de</u><u>liv</u><u>er</u>	<u>de</u><u>liv</u><u>er</u><u>ing</u>	<u>plat</u><u>form</u>
<u>pass</u><u>age</u>		

Activity Book C

Lesson 119

Activity 1

_____   _____   _____
- - - - - - - - - - - - -   - - - - - - - - - - - - -   - - - - - - - - - - - - -
_____   _____   _____
_____   _____   _____
- - - - - - - - - - - - -   - - - - - - - - - - - - -   - - - - - - - - - - - - -
_____   _____   _____
_____   _____   _____
- - - - - - - - - - - - -   - - - - - - - - - - - - -   - - - - - - - - - - - - -
_____   _____   _____
_____   _____   _____
- - - - - - - - - - - - -   - - - - - - - - - - - - -   - - - - - - - - - - - - -
_____   _____   _____

Activity 2

judge   contest   began   pie

me   giant   rules   checks

bright   spray   sprang   dry

giggle   messy   right

Lesson 119

Activity 3

_____

1. Ellen _____ in her car.

  rod   rode

2. The little _____ began to cry.

  bab   baby

3. I hear the duck _____ in the pond.

  quack   qack

4. She will _____ the contest.

  jug   judge

5. A snail is not _____.

  speedy   spedy

6. This is a _____ cat.

  cute   cut

Lesson 119

Activity 4

<u>vani</u>lla   <u>pudd</u>ing
___ __

fami<u>ly</u>   <u>gro</u>cery
___ _.   ___ _

<u>bas</u>ke<u>t</u>ball   <u>Sat</u>urday
___ ___

<u>y</u>esterday   <u>con</u>cert
__ __ __ __

<u>fly</u>ing
__ __

Lesson 120

Activity 1

ki_n_g	l_a_te	w_i_fe
h_e_r	qu_ee_n	toni_g_ht
mi_g_ht	bri_g_ht	t_ie_
dinn_e_r	t_o_ld	squ_i_re
ma_y_or	bef_o_re	sli_c_e
	du_ch_ess	

Lesson 120

Activity 2

some   oh   have   was   are   half

onto   here   what   to   heard   you

there   said   Mr.   those   says   of

away   does   one   again   tonight

would   two   could   Mrs.   out   four

want   eight   should   bear   these

water   do   hurray   I'm   today

they   were   too   once   your

oh no   pull   where   put   wrote

Lesson 120

Activity 3

princess   invite   never

duchess   tonight   reply

dinner   replied   before

    Activity Book C